BLUE-AND-YELLOW
MACAW

Nature's Green Umbrella
Tropical Rain Forests

TARSIER

SALAMANDER

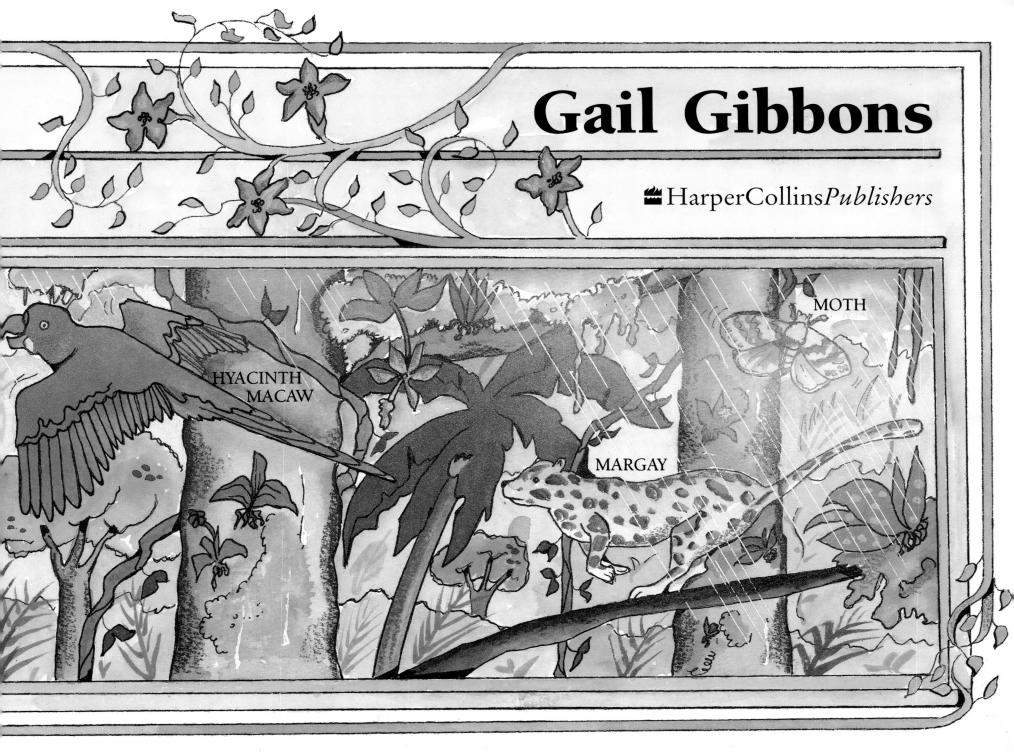

Gail Gibbons

HarperCollins*Publishers*

MOTH

HYACINTH
MACAW

MARGAY

Special thanks to James Doherty,
General Curator at the New York
Zoological Society, Bronx, New York

The illustrations in this book depict animals, trees, and plants
from tropical rain forests all over the world.

A portion of the earnings from this book is being donated for tropical rain forest preservation.

Watercolors, colored pencils, and India ink were used for the full-color artwork.
The text type is 17-point Berkeley Old Style.

Nature's Green Umbrella
Copyright © 1994 by Gail Gibbons
Manufactured in China. All rights reserved.
Library of Congress Cataloging-in-Publication Data

Gibbons, Gail.
    Nature's green umbrella: tropical rain forests / Gail Gibbons.
        p.   cm.
    Summary: Describes the climatic conditions of the rain forest as well as the
different layers of plants and animals that comprise the ecosystem.
        ISBN 0-688-12353-8 — ISBN 0-688-12354-6 (lib. bdg.)
        ISBN 0-688-15411-5 (pbk.)
    1. Rain forest ecology—Juvenile literature.   2. Rain forests—Juvenile literature.
[1. Rain forest ecology.   2. Ecology   3. Rain forests.]   I. Title.
QH541.5R27G52   1994   93-17569
574.5'2642'0913—dc20   CIP
                                                                              AC

First paperback edition, 1997

Visit us on the World Wide Web!
www.harperchildrens.com

reen leaves, wet leaves. The air is hot and steamy. Everything is moist. The skies darken and it begins to rain. It pours on nature's green umbrella, the tropical rain forest.

Most rain forests are found in warm, wet climates near the equator. These areas are called the *tropics*. When the sun shines, temperatures can reach 90 degrees Fahrenheit. They rarely fall below 70 degrees. Many tropical rain forests stay green year-round.

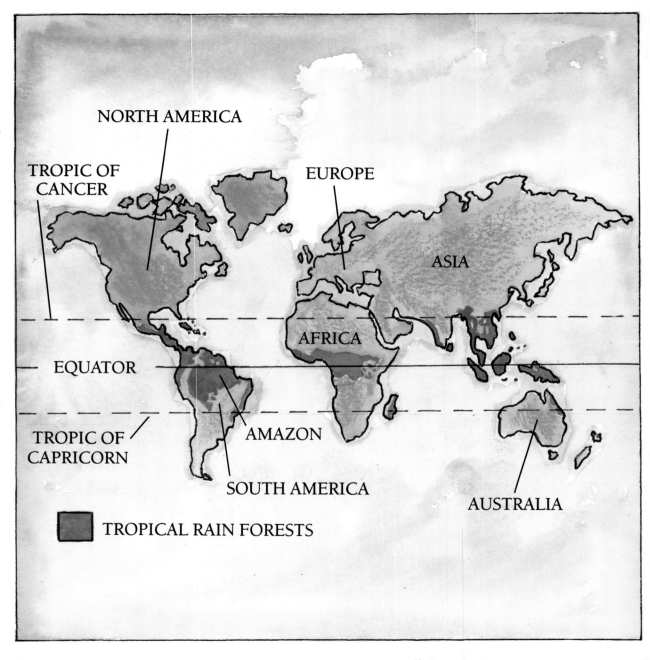

NORTH AMERICA

TROPIC OF CANCER

EUROPE

ASIA

AFRICA

EQUATOR

TROPIC OF CAPRICORN

AMAZON

SOUTH AMERICA

AUSTRALIA

TROPICAL RAIN FORESTS

Trees and plants TRANSPIRE a watery vapor into the air through their leaves.

Rain forests help create their own wet climates. They are thick with plant life. These plants and trees soak up rainwater from the soil and return it to the air through *transpiration*. About half the transpired water falls back down on the forest as rain—lots of rain! It rains more than 200 days a year in most rain forests. Sometimes as much as 240 inches of rain falls each year.

Scientists believe some tropical rain forests have existed for 100 million years. Today they cover about 7 percent of the earth's land surface. Pushed together, they would be just about the size of the United States. Living in them are at least half of the earth's *species*, or kinds, of plants and animals. Scientists are constantly discovering more. A single acre of rain forest, about the size of two football fields, may have over 300 different kinds of trees. In the United States or in Europe, a similar area of forest may have only 12 kinds. The earth's biggest rain forest is the Amazon forest in South America. It is home to more than 1600 species of birds and about a million different kinds of insects.

BUSHMASTER
SNAKE

MORPHO
BUTTERFLY

DART POISON
FROG

SPIDER
MONKEY

TOUCAN

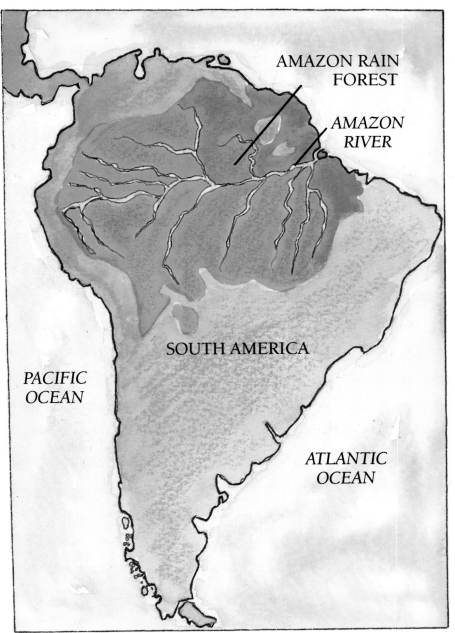

AMAZON RAIN
FOREST

AMAZON
RIVER

SOUTH AMERICA

PACIFIC
OCEAN

ATLANTIC
OCEAN

The rain forest, with its millions of plant and animal species, makes up a special community called an *ecosystem*. This term comes partly from a Greek word meaning "house" or "place." From treetop to beneath the forest floor, all parts of the ecosystem work together to make sure that the rain forest thrives. Of the many ecosystems on earth, tropical rain forests are the most complex.

BOA
CONSTRICTOR

An ECOSYSTEM is a community in nature, including all its living and nonliving parts.

JAGUAR

OXYGEN is a gas found in the atmosphere. Animals, including people, need it to breathe.

CARBON DIOXIDE is a gas released into the air when animals exhale. Cars and factories create carbon dioxide, too.

The life of all rain forest ecosystems begins with sun, air, water, and soil. Green plants take in carbon dioxide from the air and water and minerals from the soil. Their leaves contain *chlorophyll*, a substance that uses energy from the sun to turn these materials into food. During this process, called *photosynthesis*, oxygen is released into the air.

HUMMINGBIRD

ARPY
AGLE

BIGNONE LIANA

Plant life provides food for the insects and other animals that share the rain forest ecosystem. In turn, these creatures become food for the meat eaters. This is a natural part of the life cycle of the forest. When death occurs, many organisms—such as fungi and bacteria, and insects and worms—break down the tissues of rotting tree trunks, other dead plants, and animals. These tissues become *nutrients* that go back into the soil and provide food for plants and trees. The cycle of life begins again.

ORCHID

MEAT EATER

OCELOT

PLANT EATER

OKAPI

Tropical rain forests are more than fascinating ecosystems. They are important to the world's climate. We've seen that some of the water transpired by the rain forests falls back again as rain. The rest is spread by warm currents of air to cooler, drier parts of the earth.

BROMELIAD

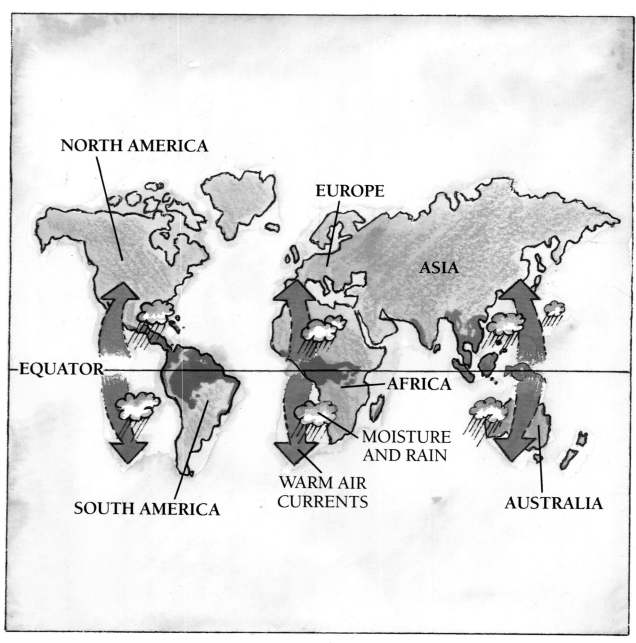

NORTH AMERICA

EUROPE

ASIA

EQUATOR

AFRICA

MOISTURE AND RAIN

WARM AIR CURRENTS

SOUTH AMERICA

AUSTRALIA

CARBON. DIOXIDE

GHOST BAT

OXYGEN

SLOTH

SCARLET MACAW

Tropical rain forests also help keep a healthy balance of gases in the air. Carbon dioxide is absorbed by the millions of trees and other plants. They in turn give off vast amounts of oxygen for people and other animals to breathe.

Although a rain forest is one ecosystem, it is made up of different layers. In each layer, the plants and animals are specially suited to their place in the ecosystem. The tallest trees, scattered throughout the rain forest, are called *emergents*. They can grow to be about 300 feet tall. They poke through the top layer of rain forest growth, called the *canopy*. The layer below the canopy is called the *understory*, and beneath that is the *forest floor*.

HIBISCUS

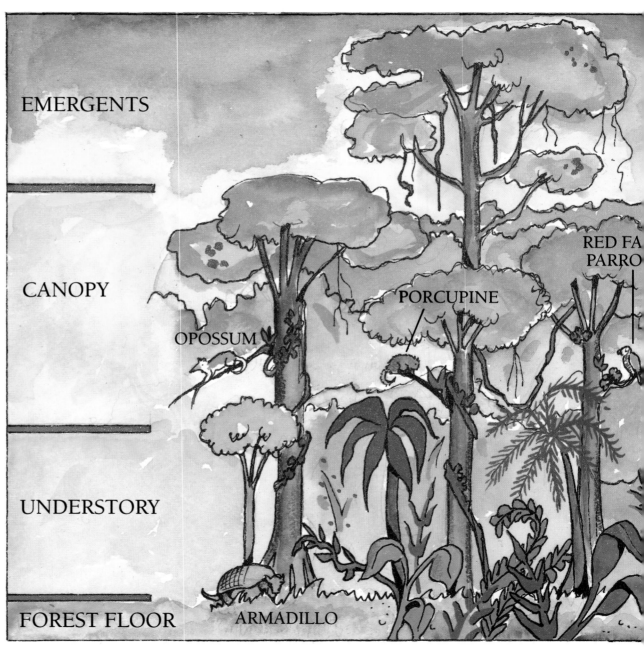

EMERGENTS

CANOPY

UNDERSTORY

FOREST FLOOR

OPOSSUM

PORCUPINE

RED FA
PARRO

ARMADILLO

THE CANOPY

Many trees in the rain forest stand between 60 and 150 feet tall. Their branches and leaves form a sort of canopy, or umbrella, that shades the forest floor. These tall trees grow so close together that rain can reach the ground only by rolling down their trunks! *Epiphytes,* or air plants, are well suited to life in the canopy. Epiphytes don't have roots in the ground to get their food. Instead, they rest on trees and live off nutrients in the wet air, taking them in through their tissues or hanging roots.

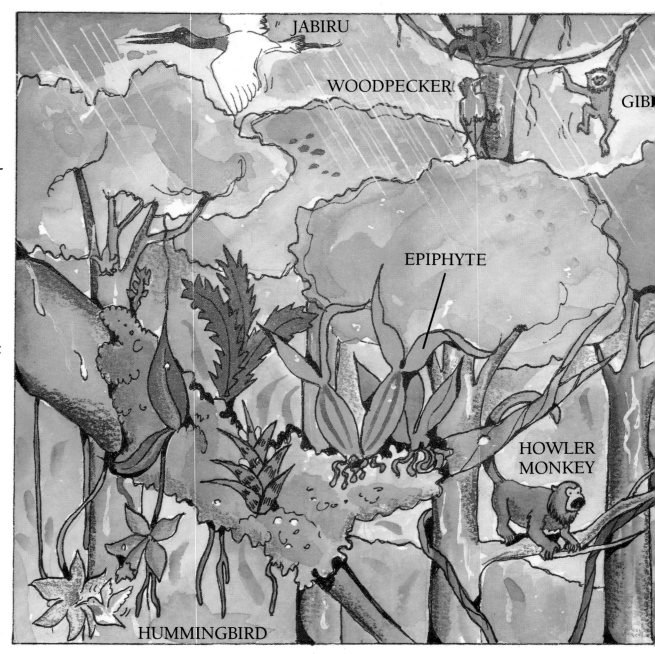

JABIRU

WOODPECKER

GIB

EPIPHYTE

HOWLER
MONKEY

HUMMINGBIRD

LONG-TONGUED BAT

EPIPHYTE

IGUANA

TREE FROG

SWALLOWBILL BUTTERFLY

The canopy is alive with activity. Air plants often have beautiful flowers that attract insects, birds, and other animals to feed on their sweet nectar. Some tree frogs spend their entire lives up in the canopy's treetops, never going down to the ground. Sticky pads on their fingers and toes help them climb around the slippery leaves.

PASSION FLOWER

THE UNDERSTORY

In the understory grow vines, smaller trees, ferns, and palms. Beneath them are still smaller bushes and ferns. Woody vines, called *lianas*, creep up and around the taller tree trunks. Spider monkeys swing from the lianas, looking for fruit to eat. It is very hot and humid, because much of the heat and moisture is trapped under the leaves of the canopy. Few flowers bloom here because of the lack of sunlight.

BIRD-OF-PARADISE

KINKAJOU

LIANA

LEAF BUTTERFLY

FERN

THE FOREST FLOOR

Only about 1 percent of the sunlight shining on the canopy filters to the ground. Here mosses, herbs, and fungi grow. Some of the plants are *parasitic*. This means they attach themselves to other plants and take away their food. The forest floor is covered with wet leaves, called *leaf litter*. Dead plants and animals rot quickly, sending nutrients back to the soil.

AMARYLLIS

PECCARY

HERBS

MOSS

FUNGI

LEAF LITTER

TARANTULA

STILT ROOTS

BUTTRESS ROOTS

ANTEATER

LEAF-CUTTING ANTS

An anteater moves around the *stilt roots* of a tall tree, looking for ants to gobble up with its long, sticky tongue. Many rain forest trees have very shallow roots. Large growths, called *buttress roots,* come out of the trunk above the ground and help support them. Stilt roots provide support, too. Below ground, the trees' roots are shallow because the soil itself isn't very rich or deep. Most tropical soils are so old that the combination of heat and rain has *leached,* or washed, much of the soil away. Nutrients are found in the thin layer of topsoil left behind.

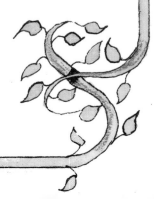

For over 40,000 years, people have lived in tropical rain forests, hunting, gathering food, and raising vegetables. They learned how to use thousands of rain forest plants for medicine. These people rarely harmed their environment because of their small numbers and the ways in which they used the rain forests.

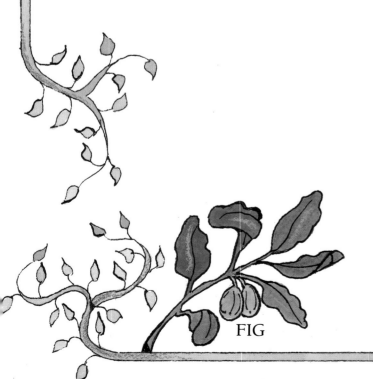

FIG

In time, other people came to the rain forests. They found wonderful foods like sweet potatoes, mangoes, and oranges, and they realized that these foods could be grown on farms and plantations and shipped all over the world.

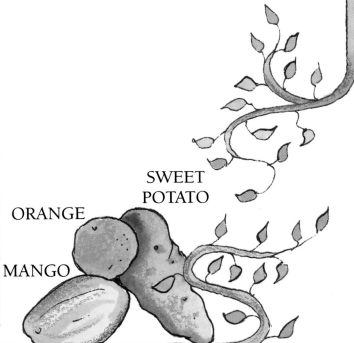

SWEET POTATO

ORANGE

MANGO

They discovered many thousands of plant varieties. About one fourth of all the medicines doctors use to cure disease come from rain forest plants. The *periwinkle*, a rain forest flower, is used to produce two drugs that help cure different types of cancer. The juice of a South American liana, called *curare*, is sometimes used to relax a patient's muscles during surgery.

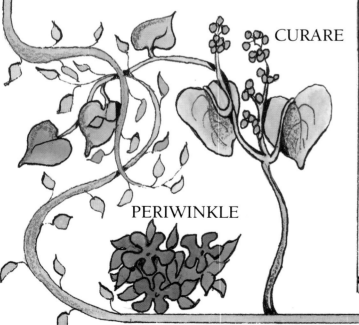

CURARE

PERIWINKLE

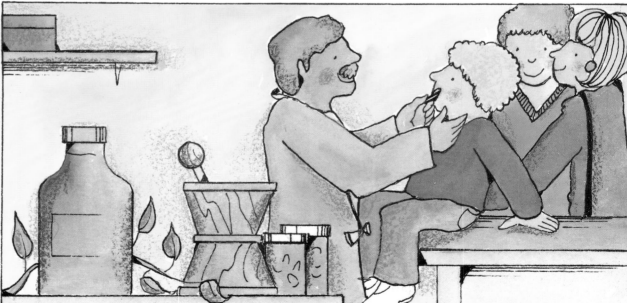

For most of their existence, the tropical rain forests were left undisturbed. Rain forest plants and animals flourished. Today many rain forests are quickly disappearing, at a rate of about 50 million acres each year worldwide. Trees are being harvested for their valuable wood. Even more are being cut down and burned to clear the land for roads, farming, and grazing. This practice is called "slash and burn."

As forests are destroyed, some people believe the earth's climate is changing. There is already a lot of carbon dioxide in the air. The burning of the rain forests releases even more. All this carbon dioxide hangs in the atmosphere with other gases that are created in similar ways. With fewer trees to take in carbon dioxide and transpire water back into the air, the earth's warmth could be trapped inside a growing layer of these gases. The world's climate could become warmer. This is called the "greenhouse effect."

Meanwhile, another threat in rain forest areas is from *flooding*. Without the protection of rain forest plants, soil is washed away by rain and wind. A useless wasteland is left behind. Without vegetation to slow the rain down, it rushes into streams and rivers, causing them to rise and flood vast areas. As the rain forests disappear, so do countless species of plants and animals.

Many people are working hard to save the tropical rain forests from destruction. They hope to protect the people who live there, too. One way is to create protected places called *reserves*. In some reserves only *selective cutting* is done. This means that loggers and farmers can cut down certain trees, but others must be left to grow. Some people think *extractive reserves* will also help. In these reserves, people are allowed to take only limited amounts of fruit, plants, nuts, latex for the production of rubber, and other natural products.

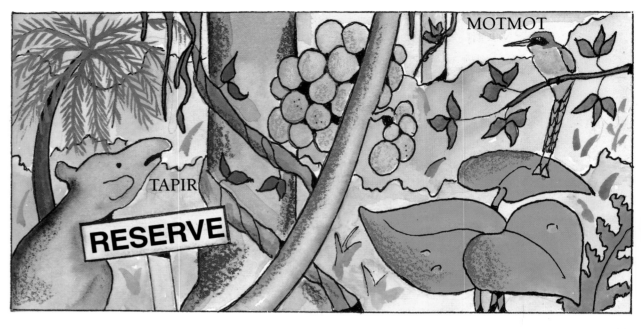

MOTMOT

TAPIR

RESERVE

SELECTIVE CUTTING RESERVE

EXTRACTIVE RESERVE

HYACINTH MACAWS

Green leaves, wet leaves. Inside the tropical rain forests, life continues where it isn't threatened. The air is thick and hot. Once again, rain falls. The survival of the tropical rain forests is important, because they are nature's green umbrella.

Different Kinds of Rain Forests

TROPICAL RAIN FORESTS

EQUATORIAL EVERGREEN FORESTS are found in the tropics near the equator. They are the wettest kind of rain forests. There is no dry season so it is always green. A rainstorm in these forests can drop as much as one inch of rain in 30 minutes!

TROPICAL MOIST FORESTS don't get as much rain as equatorial evergreen forests. Moist forests have wet and dry seasons. During dry seasons many trees lose their leaves. Trees that lose their leaves are called *deciduous* trees.

CLOUD FORESTS don't depend on rain. They are found in the mountains of the tropics. Cloud forests get their water from moisture in the clouds above them. The temperatures are cooler than in the other tropical rain forests.

MANGROVE FORESTS

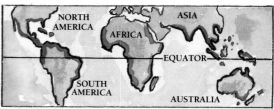

MANGROVE TREE

These are also called FLOODED FORESTS. They grow along the sea. They stay wet year-round, soaking up rainwater and seawater. Mangrove trees have long roots to hold them in place.

TEMPERATE RAIN FORESTS

These forests are not found in the tropics. Temperatures are cooler and the seasons are more distinct. Plants and animals differ from those found in tropical rain forests—for instance, "old growth trees" such as the sequoia that grow in northern California. Some of these enormous temperate rain forest trees are over 1000 years old!

SEQUOIA TREE